SYLVIA EARLE

A LERNER BIOGRAPHY

SYLVIA EARLE

Guardian of the Sea

Beth Baker

ᕃ Lerner Publications Company/Minneapolis

For Ross, Sarah, and Danny
—my favorite snorkeling partners

Lerner Publications Company
A division of Lerner Publishing Group
241 First Avenue North
Minneapolis, Minnesota 55401 U.S.A.

Website address: www.lernerbooks.com

Library of Congress Cataloging-in-Publication Data

Baker, Beth
   Sylvia Earle, guardian of the sea / by Beth Baker.
        p.   cm. — (Lerner biographies)
   Includes bibliographical references and index.
      Summary: Describes the life of this groundbreaking marine
   biologist and diver, from her childhood in New Jersey and Florida to
   her deep sea explorations of the 1980s and 1990s.
      ISBN 0-8225-4961-1 (lib. bdg. : alk. paper)
      1. Earle, Sylvia A., 1935– —Juvenile literature. 2. Marine
   biologists—United States—Juvenile literature. 3. Women marine
   biologists—United States—Juvenile literature. [1. Earle, Sylvia A.,
   1935– 2. Marine biologists. 3. Underwater exploration. 4. Deep
   diving. 5. Women Biography.] I. Title. II. Series.
   QH91.3.E2B34   2001
   578.77'092—dc21
   [B]   99–32159

Manufactured in the United States of America
1 2 3 4 5 6 – JR – 06 05 04 03 02 01

Contents

Sylvia Earle broke barriers in the advancement of ocean research and technology.

ONE

OUT OF AIR

Swimming deep beneath the surface of the Caribbean Sea, Sylvia Earle felt an unfamiliar prickle of fear when she realized she could not breathe. She had been watching a fish munching a patch of algae. Suddenly the tube leading to her scuba tank became blocked, probably with sand. She tried again to inhale. Nothing. Not yet too alarmed, she reached for the valve to release the emergency supply of air, but the valve was broken.

Trying to remain calm, she quickly estimated the distance between her and "home"—the underwater dwelling she shared with four other women the summer of 1970. Glowing like a small city at night, the twin towers of Tektite loomed a thousand feet away—too far to reach with only the air that remained in her lungs. She could have unbuckled her weight belt and thrust her body upward to the surface of the water like a rocket, but that could mean paralysis, or even death. When divers rise too rapidly to the surface of the water, a crippling burst of nitrogen bubbles can enter the bloodstream—a condition called the bends. The bends can kill a diver.

7

Instead of surfacing, Sylvia swam swiftly over to her dive partner, Peggy Lucas, who was working nearby. Knowing that every second mattered, Sylvia gave the out of air signal—a swift slicing motion with her finger across her neck. Without hesitation, Peggy removed her mouthpiece and handed it to Sylvia for a precious puff of air. After inhaling in what she hoped was a calm fashion, Sylvia passed the mouthpiece back to Peggy. In this way, the two divers shared the air supply as they swam back to their habitat. As quickly as danger came, it passed.

"The greatest threat to survival underwater, and perhaps elsewhere, is not the bends, sharks, poisonous jellies, or other imagined terrors of the deep—it's panic," Sylvia wrote later. She had never had to buddy-breathe before, but she was an experienced diver who knew how to stay calm during a crisis.

By the time Sylvia had trouble with her breathing equipment that day in 1970, she had so much experience as a diver that she could calmly react.

This was one reason Sylvia had been chosen to lead the first all-female scientific team to take part in Tektite II, one of the U.S. government's experiments in underwater living. Sylvia Earle would make history many more times in her career as a deep-sea diver and marine biologist. The more time she spent underwater, the more strongly she believed that ocean life needs protecting. She became one of the world's foremost defenders of the sea and its creatures.

Sylvia Alice Earle in Gibbstown, New Jersey, in 1936

TWO

THE BIRD LADY'S DAUGHTER

Sylvia Alice Earle was born on August 30, 1935, in the blue-collar community of Gibbstown, New Jersey. She was the second of Alice and Lewis Earle's three children.

One of her first memories was playing in the surf during the family's summer vacation when she was three years old. A great wave slammed the shore and knocked her down into a swirl of sand, water, and foam. Instead of crying, she got to her feet ready to leap joyfully into the next wave. From that moment on, Sylvia loved the ocean.

That same year, 1938, the family moved a few miles away to an old farm, just outside Paulsboro, New Jersey. The dilapidated farmhouse had been abandoned for so long that local children believed it was haunted. There was no running water, electricity, or heat. The wind moaned through cracks in the windows, and bats lived in the attic. Nevertheless, Sylvia's parents had both been raised on farms, and they wanted their children to grow up in the country too.

The house, built when George Washington was president, was made from small bricks that had been brought in the hold of an English ship as ballast, or weight, to keep it steady. The nails and beams were rough-hewn by hand, and the kitchen fireplace was so big Sylvia's father could stand in it.

Lewis, an electrician at a factory, was clever with his hands. He wired the house and installed the plumbing. After many months of hard work, the Earle family had a comfortable home, filled with plants, animals, and noisy laughter.

Sylvia's parents never had much money, but they were generous with their time and energy. When Sylvia was small, her father requested to work the night shift, so he could spend mornings with the children, tumbling around like a great big kid himself.

To Sylvia, the farm was the best place in the world, especially the outdoors. Not only was there a pond and a creek, but also an ancient orchard of gnarled trees and grape vines to explore. Alice and Lewis added apple, pear, and walnut trees and a huge garden. They raised sweet corn, tomatoes, lima beans, and slender green stalks of asparagus that Sylvia and her brothers, Lewis (Skip) and Evan, helped cut. For a summer snack, Sylvia would pluck a green pepper from the garden, lop off the top, dump the seeds, and fashion a bowl for fresh-picked mulberries. The farm's many flowers reflected all the colors of an artist's palette. Sylvia, who was small for her age, particularly liked the drooping branches of a lilac bush, under which she could hide.

Sylvia had straight, brown hair and a lively, eager face, and she was always ready for an adventure. When she was five years old, her parents heard that a pilot was coming to town, offering rides in his plane for a small fee. The family drove to a nearby field where a bright yellow Piper Cub sat

Sylvia and her father in 1936

with its propeller churning. The plane had only one passenger seat, but when Sylvia's turn came, she didn't mind climbing aboard by herself. "I do not remember any hesitation about stepping into the seat behind the pilot and being swept skyward for a few turns along the outskirts of town," she later wrote. "I *do* remember the engine noise, the exhilarating rush of air sweeping across my face and whipping my hair, and then looking down at what appeared to be dollhouses and a scattering of miniature people."

Even better than the plane ride were the family's annual treks to Ocean City, New Jersey. She and her brothers enjoyed chasing small sand crabs, collecting shells, and jumping in the waves. Sometimes they would see the sleek gray backs of dolphins rising out of the water far from shore.

There was no television when Sylvia was growing up, but she had a pony named Minnehaha, a quarter horse called Tony, a pond for ice skating, and butterflies to chase. The children spent their evenings playing board games, drawing, and reading. Sylvia's favorite books were true tales of adventure and stories about animals. At night, when she was supposed to be asleep, she would hide under the blanket with a flashlight to read the encyclopedia. In fact, throughout Sylvia's life there never were enough hours in the day to do all that she wanted.

Sylvia could often be found by the pond, involved in one of her "investigations," as her mother called them. She would sit on the roots of a willow tree, enjoying how the moist dirt felt on her bare feet. She tried to sit very still. The longer she was quiet, without waving away a bug or scratching her ankles where the grass tickled, the greater the chance that she would observe something interesting in the water. She kept a notebook at her side for sketching and writing down her observations. No one had taught Sylvia how to collect scientific data this way. It was simply an activity she enjoyed. "I always knew, somehow, that I was going to be a biologist or a botanist, even before I knew what those things were called," she later said.

The house was filled with jars of Sylvia's collections. When her Aunt Maisie came to visit, she was disgusted by the sight of tadpoles, salamanders, and insects lining the window sills. How, she demanded, could Alice allow such things in her kitchen? Alice just laughed. She was happy that her daughter loved plants and animals as much as she herself did. From the time Sylvia and her brothers were young, Alice taught them to admire the wonders outside their door—a parade of baby ducks marching behind their mother, the delicate green of a

Sylvia and her brothers sit in front of the fireplace and write their letters to Santa. From left to right: Skip, Sylvia, and Evan.

Sylvia as a young girl

giant luna moth at dusk, a hillside carpeted with violets, and on rare nights, when the sky was very clear, the spectacular display of northern lights known as the aurora borealis.

Alice's love of animals earned her quite a reputation in the neighborhood, and she became known as the Bird Lady for her gentle manner and healing skills. Children brought Alice injured birds and animals to treat because she had been a nurse. At one time, Alice nursed four orphan squirrels that Sylvia remembered as little balls of fluff. First Alice fed the squirrels with an eye dropper. Then she showed Sylvia and her brothers how to feed the squirrels small pieces of bread dipped in milk—and later dipped in peanut butter. In a few weeks, they set the squirrels free to make their own way on the farm.

On autumn days, Sylvia and her mother took walks around the farm. Alice sometimes looked up at the sky and sadly remarked that the birds were disappearing. She didn't know why, but the number of birds that used to fly overhead during the spring and autumn migration was dwindling. Sylvia remembered a dozen little songbirds she had come across—all dead—and wondered what had happened to them.

Sylvia began to sense a change in the air. More and more, her mother had to nurse Evan, who was frequently ill with bronchitis and pneumonia. Alice sat by Evan's side as he coughed painfully. Her father, too, was having troubles at the factory.

Sylvia and her family around the time they left their farm in New Jersey. From left to right: Sylvia's father and mother, Skip, Sylvia, Evan, and their dog Star.

THREE

"My Backyard Was the Gulf of Mexico"

When Sylvia was 12 years old, her father's unhappiness with his job and her brother's ill health led to a move to Florida, a thousand miles away from her beloved farm. "I didn't want to move at all," Sylvia recalled. "The woods, the pond, and fields were part of what I regarded as me." But her father decided to start an electrical contracting business near his brother's home, and her mother thought the change in climate would help Evan.

On a summer day in 1948, the Earle family said good-bye to the farm and piled into the car for their move to Dunedin, a small town north of Clearwater, Florida. After several days on the road, they drove down a dead-end street. Sylvia knew the new house was near the water, but she still was not prepared for what she saw. Spreading out like a magic carpet was a giant expanse of sea. "My backyard was the Gulf of Mexico," she said. Sylvia felt an unexpected thrill. Unlike the brooding gray Atlantic in which she had played every summer, the sea here was turquoise, warm, and calm. "That's when she lost her heart to the water," her mother said.

When Sylvia's family moved to Florida, she had the chance to swim with sea horses and other marine creatures.

For her birthday that year, Sylvia's parents gave her a simple pair of swim goggles, a gift she always remembered. With the new goggles, she began her investigations again and was richly rewarded. Floating on the surface, she peered down at tiny crabs scurrying beneath her. Scallops burrowed in the sand, with only a telltale bump and blush of color to betray them. Hundreds of little fish darted through the grassy water. To Sylvia's amazement, an occasional sea horse floated by, looking like a miniature replica of Tony, the horse she'd left behind. "Having a chance to get acquainted with new critters was really a very good thing. It softened the blow of leaving the farm," Sylvia said.

She gradually grew accustomed to her new home. Sylvia and her brothers explored the town of Dunedin. Stately oak trees lined the main avenues, forming a shady canopy. The children roamed the five-and-dime and bought nickel Coca-Colas at the Blue Bird Drug Store's soda fountain.

Sylvia soon discovered the town library. She loved sea adventures, and her favorite author was William Beebe. He was a biologist who had invented a way to descend deep into the

William Beebe was Sylvia's favorite author. She wanted to see the many creatures he wrote about.

ocean in a round chamber called a bathysphere in the 1920s. In *Half-Mile Down* he wrote: "In this kingdom most of the plants are animals, the fish are friends, colors are unearthly in their shift and delicacy; here miracles become marvels, and marvels recurring wonders. There may be a host of terrible dangers, but in hundreds of dives we have never encountered them." The words thrilled Sylvia. She longed to see the extraordinary creatures that Beebe described.

She and her brothers spent hours playing in the water. Sometimes Skip wanted to swim races. He had a fine stroke, and his arms cut cleanly through the water's surface. Sylvia tried to copy his smooth style, but she could not compete with him. Underwater was another story, however. There, she glided like a fish.

Sylvia's interest in nature continued to grow. In ninth grade, her science teacher, Edna Turnure, gave Sylvia great encouragement. "I loved doing special reports and making drawings of creatures and of my observations. I always had tons of extra credit," she remembered.

Sylvia's closest friend was Peggy MacKenzie, who lived in a little house near the water. Sylvia walked to Peggy's house through a woods of palmetto and pine trees. Sometimes the two girls set out in their inner tubes to St. Joseph's Sound, one mile north in the Gulf. One day as they drifted home, they noticed that something was churning the water, making it dull and cloudy. They followed the ugly path to a pipe jutting from a new orange juice factory. The plant was dumping orange pulp into the clear water.

The orange juice factory was not the only unwelcome change from Sylvia's viewpoint. Dunedin was becoming a bustling town. The beautiful old oak trees were being cut down. New hotels were being erected, and a sea wall was being built to protect the new property from water damage. Sylvia wondered what would happen to the sea grasses and the tiny animals that lived there.

As the end of high school drew near, Sylvia grew restless. She had good grades, but she felt there were more important things she wanted to do. She was anxious to get on with her life.

Sylvia enjoys studying marine life in the lab as well as in the ocean.

FOUR

THE MAKING OF A MARINE SCIENTIST

Among the reeds deep in the Weekiwatchee River, an alligator gar fixed its gaze on Sylvia. The big fish opened and closed its long, narrow jaw, displaying its wicked set of teeth. When it turned and slid away, Sylvia wanted to follow, but the whooshing rush of the river's powerful current nearly knocked her over.

For 16-year-old Sylvia, the fish seemed like an exotic gatekeeper awaiting her as she first tried breathing underwater. A school friend had invited Sylvia and Skip to try out some diving gear. The boy's father used the gear to dive for sponges, a common occupation along the Gulf of Mexico.

When her turn came, Sylvia slipped a heavy copper helmet over her head, its sharp edge digging into her shoulders. The helmet was attached by a hose to an air compressor on land. Each breath she took underwater would be of compressed air—air that had been squeezed and put under pressure. Without this kind of air in her lungs, she would be crushed by the vast weight of the water pushing down on her.

Plunging into the water, Sylvia paddled downward, but she soon felt a jolt of pain in her ears from the pressure of the water. After she swallowed repeatedly, the pain eased and she began to enjoy her adventure.

When Sylvia stood on the bottom of the river, 30 feet beneath the surface, she carefully edged her way out of the strong current. Suddenly she spotted a school of small, golden fish. Like a scout stalking deer in the forest, she slowly approached the fish. Rather than darting away, as she had expected, the fish swam to her. It was just as William Beebe had written: "The joy of it all is that everything that moves has little or no fear of us. We are made to feel at home—returning natives, not intruding strangers."

After 20 minutes, Sylvia's vision began to blur and she felt faint. Just as she was tugging on the hose to signal she wanted

Sylvia was fascinated with all kinds of marine life.

to come up, one of her friends dove down to get her. The pump for the compressed air was not working properly. Sylvia was breathing a deadly blend of carbon monoxide and other gases. Her friends hauled her onto the riverbank just in time.

When Sylvia took her first underwater breath in 1952, deep-sea exploration was advancing rapidly. A decade earlier, captain Jacques Cousteau and engineer Emile Gagnan had invented the aqualung, later known as scuba (self-contained underwater breathing apparatus). In his book *The Silent World,* Cousteau had described his adventures exploring caves and sunken ships and swimming with seals and sharks. Sylvia loved the book. She imagined herself flying through the water like Cousteau—but not shooting fish with a spear gun as he had done.

Jacques Cousteau invented a new type of diving equipment called scuba.

Sylvia's chance to try the new diving equipment came sooner than she had expected. When she was 17, she took a summer marine biology course at Florida State University. Her instructor was Dr. Harold J. Humm, whose love of the marine world deeply inspired Sylvia. Instead of bringing up plants and animals to stick under a microscope, Dr. Humm urged his students to go and see them as they live.

On their first field trip, Sylvia eagerly surveyed Dr. Humm's equipment. There were glass-bottom buckets, face masks and flippers, an air compressor, and most exciting to Sylvia, two scuba tanks, just as Jacques Cousteau had used! The sleek new device was a big improvement over the clunky copper helmet she had first tried.

Sylvia on the beach in 1956

Sylvia explored the sea without fear. Those around her could see her enthusiasm for the world that existed in the deep waters.

On a boat, Dr. Humm took the students five miles off the shore of St. Mark's Wildlife Refuge. His instructions for using the scuba tanks were simple: "Breathe naturally." Holding your breath while inhaling compressed air was dangerous. The air could expand and cause pain or even death as the diver rose to the surface.

Without fear, Sylvia jumped off the boat into a bed of sea grass. "With a gentle kick I glided to a small clump of sponges and found a feisty three-inch-long damselfish who was not pleased by my intrusion into its territory. Balancing myself with one finger, I found it easy literally to do a headstand so that I could peer into the dark crevices of the fish's lair," she wrote.

Sylvia wished she could spend her life scuba diving. She wondered if she could follow in Dr. Humm's footsteps and teach marine biology. For a teenage girl in the 1950s, this was an unusual career choice. The most common occupations for women were nurse, secretary, airline hostess, and teacher. Of these choices, Sylvia was able to imagine herself becoming a teacher, especially if she could be like Dr. Humm and spend time in the water.

"I remember her unusual enthusiasm," Dr. Humm said many years later. "She showed a dedication to marine science, even at that young age. She had an exceptional ability to learn and to retain what she learned."

Sylvia studied hard, first at St. Petersburg Junior College and then at Florida State University. When she decided to pursue her master's degree, she was accepted at many top universities—Yale, Cornell, and Duke among them. Duke, however, offered Sylvia two things she could not refuse—a full scholarship and a chance to continue her studies under Dr. Humm, who was then teaching there.

Alice and Lewis, still living in Dunedin, were very proud of their daughter's success. Alice began to baby-sit for children in the neighborhood, sending her earnings to Sylvia to pay for her food. Sometimes Alice would send care packages of homemade skirts, blouses, and dresses. "I was the best-dressed person in school," Sylvia said proudly.

With her parents' encouragement and her own boundless energy, Sylvia began to believe she could become a scientist. During her two years at Duke, Sylvia decided to major in botany, the study of plant life. She focused on algae in particular. Although some people think of algae as green scum or slimy seaweed, Sylvia found it amazing. "You'd have a hard time imagining plants so bizarre and absolutely magnificent. Algae could inspire poets and songwriters," she said.

There are hundreds of types of algae. *Rhodophyta* is red seaweed that thrives in warm coastal waters. Blue-green algae, an ancient form of life, nurtured other plants and animals on Earth long ago. Other algae, called diatoms, look like tiny glass jewel boxes. Some of Sylvia's favorites have a special property, called bioluminescence, which allows them to send off their own light like fireflies. To learn about the

Sylvia spent hours studying the plants underwater. Algae, shown above and at top, were some of the many objects of Sylvia's studies.

Red reef shrimp, shown here at night, were some of the many colorful creatures Sylvia came across while diving.

plants, she spent many hours underwater. As she swam, she surveyed a magical world with shapes that resembled miniature fans, trees, spaghetti, and cacti. "I became enchanted with exploring them," she said.

One thing clouded Sylvia's time at Duke, however. Not everyone welcomed women in the ranks of science. She was often the only woman in her classes. When she applied for a teaching assistant position, she was told that she would not be offered the job because such an opportunity would be wasted on a female student, who "everybody knew" would end up becoming a housewife. Sylvia was indignant. She needed the money for her living expenses and books. How dare members of the faculty imply she was not serious about her studies?

Fortunately, other faculty members admired Sylvia's tough determination and intelligence. They created a new job for her in the herbarium, where plant specimens are kept.

During this time, Sylvia decided that she did not want to be a teacher. "I wanted to do something that was different, something special," she said. "I had the impression that teachers taught about what others had done. But I wanted to be the doer. I wanted to do the finding, not just learn about what others had found."

Sylvia not only wore a graduation gown but also her flippers and goggles when she graduated in 1961 with a Ph.D. from Duke University.

FIVE

AGE OF DISCOVERY

At age 20, soon after Sylvia received her master's degree, she married a young zoologist named John (Jack) Taylor. After living briefly in Live Oak and Gainesville, Sylvia and Jack moved to Dunedin, next door to Alice and Lewis.

Even though Sylvia was married, she had no intention of giving up her dream of being a marine biologist. "I could no more imagine not being a scientist than not having a backbone," she said. "It holds me together."

Sylvia and Jack turned their garage into a laboratory with a microscope and cabinets to hold the specimens they found. Sylvia planned to get a Ph.D. (Doctor of Philosophy) degree through Duke University. Her research topic was algae found in the Gulf of Mexico. From the marshy grasses of Mississippi's coast to the turquoise waters of the Florida Keys, she collected samples, measuring the temperature and salinity (saltiness) of the water, recording the depth and tides, and observing which plants and animals lived together.

In 1960, Sylvia and Jack's first child was born. Elizabeth was an active girl with strawberry blond hair. Two years later came baby John, whom the family called Richie, after Alice's maiden name. Sylvia took the children along on excursions in her boat. "Many times four small hands helped me arrange plant specimens on stiff, white sheets of herbarium paper and place them carefully between sheets of cardboard and blotting paper for drying," she wrote. This was a satisfying and peaceful time for Sylvia. She had her research, her children and husband, and her beloved parents.

Then, in August 1964, she received an unusual invitation. A research ship called the *Anton Bruun* was touring the world for the National Science Foundation. The ship was about to leave on an expedition to the Indian Ocean when one of the botanists who had planned to be aboard was unable to go. Dr. Harold Humm recommended Sylvia as a replacement.

She had every excuse to say no. Elizabeth and Richie needed her, she was studying for her exam to be accepted into the doctoral program, and her research in the Gulf of Mexico was going well. But her husband and parents assured her that they would take care of the children during her six-week absence. Dr. Humm said she could take her exam early, and the Gulf of Mexico—well, it would still be there, waiting to be explored.

Sylvia decided to go on the expedition, but the *Anton Bruun's* chief scientist told her that not everyone was happy about a woman being on board. A few of the men still believed an old superstition that women on a ship brought bad luck. Others thought the idea of one woman traveling with 70 men was not a good idea. But telling Sylvia she couldn't or shouldn't do something just because she was a woman always backfired. She became more determined than ever to achieve her goal.

Dr. Harold Humm recommended Sylvia for the adventure on the Anton Bruun. Sylvia and Dr. Humm are shown in 1965.

As she packed her bag for the journey, four-year-old Elizabeth followed her around the house, asking her mother to repeat the names of the places she was going— Mombasa, the Amirante Islands, the Aldabras, the Comores, Dar-as-Salaam. The names sounded mysterious and beautiful.

From the moment she walked on board, Sylvia knew she had to prove herself to the men. She was determined to work hard and to keep a sense of humor. For Sylvia, working hard meant doing what she loved best—exploring the sea. During the cruise she got by on very little sleep. She rose at 5:00 in the morning to begin diving and often worked into the night, writing her observations in her journal at 3:00 A.M.

In unexpected ways, being the only woman on board had its advantages. For example, she was given her own small room, while most of the men had to share sleeping space. The men viewed her as the ship's "social ambassador." When the *Anton Bruun* docked at ports, Sylvia was invited to go ashore, along with the captain and the chief scientist, to meet with dignitaries. She would have preferred spending that time in the water, but she gained valuable experience as a spokesperson.

As much as possible, though, Sylvia was underwater seeing new critters, as she called them. As she swam over tide pools, coral reefs, and mounds of black volcanic rock, she saw clown anemone fish, giant sea cucumbers, yellow butterfly fish, even a tiny octopus.

Once she came upon rocks covered "with a miniature forest of bright pink plants that appeared to have been designed by Dr. Seuss." She had never seen anything like it. The tiny plants looked like flamingo-colored palm trees or umbrellas turned inside out. Sylvia had discovered a red alga. As the discoverer, she later got to give the alga its scientific name. She called it *Hummbrella hydra,* as a funny way to describe its umbrella shape and to honor Dr. Humm.

Over the next two years, she went on four more expeditions aboard the *Anton Bruun.* As her experience grew, she would have been a logical choice to become the chief scientist aboard, but many men still resisted the idea of a woman being their leader. "I decided I could either fret and get angry and bluster my way in. Or I could relax and enjoy the circumstances. I chose to not waste energy, but to do the best job I could," she said.

During this time, Sylvia got to know Eugenie Clark, a famous scientist known as the Shark Lady. In Dr. Clark, Sylvia found a role model. Here was a woman who was a top re-

The crew members of the 1964 voyage of the Anton Bruun

searcher with her own lab and was also a wife and the mother of four children. Sylvia was a frequent visitor to Dr. Clark's lab. The women often went diving together, Sylvia looking for algae and Eugenie collecting creatures for her lab. They used a small collecting boat with a well in the middle filled with sea water to keep fish and shellfish alive.

Sylvia faced many challenges as the only woman aboard the Anton Bruun. *Here, she relaxes on the deck of the ship.*

Eugenie Clark thought that "Sylvia was extremely sweet, yet aggressive. She was so pleasant, everyone liked her. But when she wanted to do something, she went after it."

When Dr. Clark moved to New York in 1965, she asked Sylvia to be temporary director of her lab in Sarasota, which Sylvia was until 1967. During this period, Sylvia earned her Ph.D. from Duke. The lab later expanded to include the Mote Marine Aquarium, an important center for shark research.

Sylvia and her team of aquanauts swim off the U.S. Virgin Islands in July 1970.

SIX

TEKTITE II:
SOMERSAULTING
IN THE DEEP

Sylvia and her children moved to Boston after her nine years of marriage to John Taylor ended in divorce. She married Giles Mead, a leading ichthyologist (fish biologist) at Harvard University, and led a busy life. Between them, Sylvia and Giles Mead had six children—Elizabeth and Richie, three of Mead's children from a previous marriage, and a new baby, Gale, born in 1968.

The following year, 1969, the U.S. government began a series of experiments to study life in the sea. The first experiment, called Tektite I, involved four scientists who lived for two months in a special laboratory on the floor of the ocean, 50 feet below the surface.

The Tektite project was not intended to learn only about marine life. The National Aeronautics and Space Administration (NASA) also hoped to apply some of the research in outer space. Aquanauts, as sea explorers are called, and astronauts faced similar challenges—living in close quarters and exploring alien environments. The name "Tektite" expressed this sea-space connection. Tektites are green, glassy balls found on the ocean floor. Many scientists believe that tektites fell from space.

Sylvia learned about Tektite II from an announcement tacked on a bulletin board at Harvard, asking scientists to submit proposals for underwater research. The planners of Tektite, however, did not expect women would be among the scientists who applied. In those days, the idea of men and women living together in a science lab seemed improper. NASA also was less interested in having women be part of the experiment, since all the astronauts at that time were men. (It would be 13 more years—1983—before Sally Ride went on a space mission as the first U.S. female astronaut.)

But several qualified women wanted to participate. Sylvia's application was particularly impressive. Not only was she a Harvard Research Fellow, but she had more diving experience—a thousand hours at that time—than any other applicant. The planners decided to ask Sylvia to lead an all-female team.

Although it would be hard for Sylvia to get away, she didn't want to miss the opportunity Tektite presented. As always, Alice and Lewis offered to help watch the children.

Newspapers made a great fuss over the all-female team. The front page of the *Boston Globe* carried the headline: "Beacon Hill Housewife to Lead Team of Female Aquanauts."

Sylvia groaned. Ten years of research to get her doctoral degree, deep-sea expeditions around the globe, and she was seen first and foremost not as a scientist, but a housewife. Her disappointment quickly evaporated, however, as the news sunk in—two whole weeks underwater!

Sylvia and the women chosen for the Tektite mission had to go through many hours of training to participate.

Soon she was sitting at a kitchen table, 50 feet under the sea. The carpeted room, painted a cheerful aquamarine, had a television and tape deck. Each bunk bed had a curtain that could be pulled closed for a bit of privacy. Tucked into the round walls were a clothes dryer, refrigerator, and stove. NASA provided frozen meals for the crew. To decorate the room, the women made a mobile of Earth, adorned with antipollution messages. Large extended portholes gave a fish-eye view of the marine world surrounding the dwelling, and fish sometimes stopped to gaze through the lit windows.

Up a ladder from the living area was the work station, equipped with a laboratory and a communications panel. A short tunnel leading to the other side of the dwelling held the life-support system and a ladder down to a special chamber that opened to the sea. Despite its cozy interior, from the outside the habitat looked grim—like twin oil tanks, standing upright on a concrete slab with cables running to shore for communication and air. For seven months in 1970, the dwelling sat off the shore of the U.S. Virgin Islands.

The women's team, called Mission 6, was one of 10 Tektite II missions. Sylvia and her team members—biologists Dr. Renate Schlenz True and Alina Szmant, ecologist Ann Hurley, and habitat engineer Peggy Lucas—each had her own work to accomplish during their two-week stay.

As the engineer, Peggy was seeing how the dwelling might be improved. Renate wanted to learn if marine organisms would adapt to an artificial bed of plastic grass that might be useful for fish farming. Ann and Alina studied the behavior of a species called blue chromis damselfish. Sylvia's project was to survey plant species growing in the reef and learn how algae were affected by grazing fish, such as the beautiful parrotfish.

The first day was difficult. The women had to adjust to NASA psychologists monitoring them 24 hours a day from television screens topside. Every six minutes, each team member's activity was reported. Sylvia was soon struck by the humor of so many pairs of eyes watching each other—NASA watching the women, who were watching the fish, who were watching the women, who in turn could return NASA's gaze through the two-way television system.

By the second day, Sylvia was too excited about her work to be bothered by the ever-present eyes. As the new kid on the undersea block, Sylvia was eager to meet her neighbors in the blue world outside. She hoped the presence of humans would not change life on the reef, so she was pleased to see

Sylvia conducting research aboard the Tektite

sponges, algae, and worms clinging to the outside of the habitat, as if the concrete and metal hulk were a normal part of the community.

The predawn darkness was a favorite time for the team to venture out. The women clambered down the ladder to the hatch, donning their diving equipment—a weight belt to keep them from floating to the surface, a compass, watch, depth gauge, knife, strobe light, yellow emergency balloon, lantern, camera, collecting bag, waterproof writing slate, two tanks of air, flippers, face mask, and mouthpiece. All this gear somehow was strapped around their waists, ankles, wrists, and backs or held in their hands. When everyone was ready, Sylvia alerted topside that the women were setting out.

At last, they were free to enter the tropical sea, the usually warm waters chilled from night's darkness. The women swam quietly, their way lit only by small flashlights. On a typical morning, Sylvia headed for a spot where she could observe damselfish guarding their eggs. At first, all was still. But as daylight filtered down, several small damselfish, sprinkled with brilliant blue spots, cautiously came out from a coral patch where they had been resting. Dozens of slender garden eels greeted the dawn by pushing small black noses out of their burrows in the sand. Extending their bodies upward, they waved as gently as sea grass in the currents.

Other early risers included five gray angelfish—handsome round fish marked with a honeycomb of black on gray—that emerged each morning from the same crevice. What Sylvia appreciated most about living underwater was the chance to become familiar with individual fish and observe how they behaved. This was a whole new way of doing research. The hour passed quickly and the air in the scuba tanks ran low. As they returned to the habitat, Sylvia wrote, "Our sense of freedom and delight is so great that along the way we do somersaults, rolls, and loops."

One by one they swam into the pressurized chamber and climbed up the ladder to unload their gear. As they took turns bathing in the freshwater shower, Sylvia let topside know that all were back safely.

After a short rest, Sylvia would grow fidgety. Every minute spent out of water seemed like a waste of time. One afternoon, she and Renate set out, using the newly invented "rebreathers" rather than traditional scuba tanks. The new device circulated the diver's air and removed dangerous carbon dioxide. Rebreathers took longer to prepare for use, but they had many advantages. With rebreathers divers could explore

The Tektite II all-female team in rebreather training

for four glorious hours, enough time to accomplish what would take three separate trips with scuba gear. The rebreather was quieter than scuba because the device made no bubbles. The women could hear the full chorus of sounds from the sea—"the crunch of parrotfish teeth on coral, the sizzle and pop of snapping shrimp, the grunts of groupers, the chattering staccato of squirrelfish," Sylvia wrote.

That afternoon, the first stop was Renate's field of plastic grass. Algae covered the artificial strands, a good sign that fish might soon be grazing there. The two women next glided over the smooth sandy plain to one of Sylvia's study areas. Sitting on round rocks, they watched the action on the reef. Just then, a small, snakelike lizardfish swam near, then rested on Sylvia's flipper.

Sylvia displays samples to engineer Peggy Lucas inside Tektite.

Later they spotted a batfish, an odd-looking, sand-colored animal with armlike flippers for walking on the ocean floor. To her surprise, the batfish allowed Sylvia to cup it in her palm. When the fish began to wriggle, she let it swim away.

Frequently, the women swam at night. Swimming in the pitch-black sea might frighten most people, but it offered the aquanauts a chance to see a different cast of characters. Darkness brought out the octopus, which changed colors from brown to blue-green as it hunted its prey. Gleaming organisms winked like fireflies in the darkness, and moonlight shone on the ocean floor. Once a roving shadow drew Sylvia's eyes upward. A school of tarpon glided overhead like silvery torpedoes. "I was suddenly reminded of swans I had seen on a winter night, streaming across a moonlit sky," she wrote.

Far too soon, the two weeks were up. Sylvia and Ann swam out together to say farewell to the reef. As if on cue, the five gray angelfish appeared. The women harvested some algae to bring back to the doorway of the dwelling. Placing the algae on the seafloor, they waited to see if any fish would take advantage of this easy breakfast. Sylvia held back one sprig as a sample for her collection. Soon, parrotfish showed up to graze on the pile of algae. Then an angelfish came and—to Sylvia's delight—began eating the piece she held in her hand.

Reluctantly, the women began their final swim to the diving bell that awaited them. The bell brought them to a large

Swimming in the darkness at night allowed Sylvia to see creatures that may not be out during the day.

decompression chamber at the surface, where they waited for 21 hours while their bodies readjusted to the normal atmospheric pressure on land—a small price to pay, Sylvia felt, for the rare privilege of living underwater.

Sylvia's research had gone well. She had documented 154 species of marine plants, including 26 species never seen before in the Virgin Islands. She had also made new observations about the day and night behaviors of many plant-eating fish. The other team members were also pleased with what they had learned. Renate's bed of plastic grass created a good habitat for fish. Ann and Alina learned more about the escape behaviors of the blue chromis damselfish, and Peggy found the living quarters were well designed, although the laboratory space was too small.

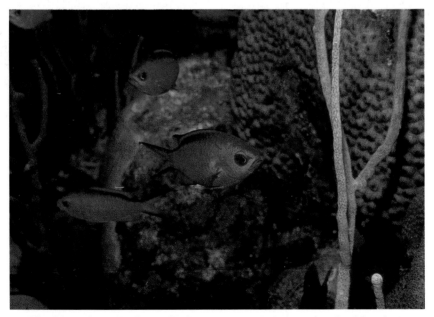

The blue chromis damselfish was one species researched by the Tektite crew.

The Tektite team

Meanwhile, reporters, enthralled with the idea of the all-female team, eagerly awaited the group's return to shore. While previous Tektite missions barely caused a ripple of attention, an enthusiastic crowd applauded when the women stepped onto the pier. As cameras snapped, each team member was given a bouquet of red roses, but that was just the beginning.

The women addressed Congress and received Conservation Service awards. First Lady Pat Nixon invited them to lunch at the White House. They rode in a parade through Chicago in a fur-lined limousine (originally made for the Pope's visit) to a reception at the Shedd Aquarium, where the famous gospel singer Mahalia Jackson sang for them.

Sylvia's attitude about sea life was one of amazement. She felt if more people could experience what she did, they would care more about protecting the ocean.

For a scientist, the sudden fame was both embarrassing and exhilarating—embarrassing because none of the other Tektite scientists had been treated that way. And the headline writers dreamed up silly names for the team, such as "aquanettes," "aquabelles," and "aquababes." Although the male scientists wouldn't have wanted to be called such silly names, some of them resented all the attention the women received.

Sylvia's reputation as a respected scientist seemed in danger of drowning in a media wave, but at the same time something important was happening. Television personalities like Barbara Walters and Hugh Downs wanted to interview her, and she received many requests for speaking engagements.

She was honest enough to recognize that her scientific expertise was not her primary appeal. The fact that she was a "girl" explorer was what made her popular with the press. If this gave her a way to reach millions of people with her message, however, then so be it. As microphones were thrust before her, she searched for the right words to express how deeply she felt about life in the oceans. Her role as a public champion of the seas had begun.

"I'm changed forever because I lived underwater for two weeks in 1970. I wish that everybody could go live underwater if only for a day," she later said. She was convinced that the more people knew about life in the sea—not just by reading about it, but by seeing it for themselves—the more they would value it. It was the "magnitude of our ignorance," she often said, that was the biggest threat to the marine environment.

The 1970s were to Sylvia a decade of great discovery and optimism. She imagined that marine biology students of the near future would study in underwater laboratories, and she was sure an exciting era of exploration was about to begin.

In 1977 Sylvia and a crew began a project to learn more about humpback whales.

SEVEN

GENTLE GIANTS

Sylvia sat poised on the edge of a small rubber boat, her heart in her throat. Below her, in the warm waters off Hawaii, swam some of the largest animals in the world, humpback whales. In 1977 few people had had the courage to swim with creatures so enormous they could easily kill a fragile human with a casual stroke of a flipper or tail.

"With more uncertainty than I have felt in thousands of dives, I eased into the water," she later wrote. As her eyes adjusted, a black form came hurtling toward her like a locomotive. For one frightening moment, she wondered if she'd made a terrible mistake. Here she was just five feet tall and one hundred pounds, up against a 40-foot, 80 thousand-pound whale. A collision seemed certain. But the whale gracefully slid past her, tilting its gigantic head to get a better look at this bold little visitor. Sylvia felt a thrill of recognition, as if she had met a kindred spirit who shared her curiosity and joy.

She turned to find her dive partners, photographers Al Giddings and Chuck Nicklin. She realized Giddings was about to have an even closer encounter with the same whale. Intent on taking a picture, Giddings had no idea that the whale was heading right for him. There was no way Sylvia could warn him. But again, at the last second, the whale swam just over Al's head. "I stopped worrying then and have never worried since in all my encounters with humpbacks," she wrote in *National Geographic.*

Humans have hunted whales for centuries, but before 1880, only about 50 whales were killed each year. Modern technology brought whaling to frightening levels. By the 1930s, more than 50,000 whales were killed annually. Harpoons were no longer flung by hand but were tipped with explosives and fired from guns. Factory ships chugged out to sea, where whales could be more efficiently butchered and ground into animal feed, lard, and cosmetics. "In less than a century we have traded 60 million years of history for margarine and cat food," Sylvia wrote. Much of the whale hunt has been banned, but many species—including the humpbacks—are still endangered.

Although human hunters know every ounce of a dead whale, little is known about living whales. Roger and Katy Payne are two scientists who worked to change that situation. After years of research, the Paynes learned that humpback whales compose elaborate songs that change each year, songs that are shared by other whales in the pod, or group.

Sylvia met Roger Payne at a conference, and they decided to collaborate on a research project. The highlight of the project would be a film made by Al Giddings, a pioneer in underwater photography. Sylvia was delighted. She and Giddings shared a fearless passion for underwater explo-

Sylvia with Roger and Katy Payne

ration, and they had worked together on many expeditions around the world. To raise money for the whale project, they approached scientific organizations, magazines, and conservation groups. They explained that very few scientists had conducted whale research by swimming alongside the giant animals, and they convinced several organizations to provide financial support.

In February 1977, they began the project in Hawaii, where humpback whales migrate in the winter. By the second day of filming, the whales already seemed to expect the crew to show up. Five black forms reversed direction and approached the boat. Without hesitation this time, Sylvia plunged in and two whales immediately swam to her from below.

The crew followed the humpbacks for three months. Sylvia learned to recognize individual whales by particular markings on the faces, flippers, underbellies, and flukes (tails).

One of the most exciting days came when the crew crossed the Alenuihaha Channel, which runs between two Hawaiian Islands. The channel is a difficult place for boats to cross. Winds blow fiercely there, and the current is strong. That day was stormy, and the swells in the sea were 30 feet high. Everyone clung to the boat as towers of water rose and fell around them. Just then, they saw an unusual sight: pygmy killer whales were interacting with the humpbacks. Despite the dreadful seas—and the fact that no one had ever swum with the aggressive pygmy killer whales—Al and Sylvia decided to go in the water to film them.

Roger Payne remembered the scene this way:

> It's utter turmoil. Everything is violent, and you can't see where water and air begin. The second Sylvia and Al went into the water, you couldn't see their bubbles [from their scuba tanks] at all. The waves were breaking into the boat, and it was absolute chaos.
>
> They made five dives. After the third dive, they came up to change a piece of equipment, and Sylvia said to Al, "Did you see those sharks?" It was so casual—she hardly mentioned it. That electrified everybody on board.

Two large, ocean white-tipped sharks had approached Sylvia in a menacing way. When one circled her, then moved in as if to attack, Sylvia gave a sharp kick of her flippers, and the shark swam away.

Roger Payne continued: "Did Sylvia and Al go back in?

Sylvia encountered ocean white-tipped sharks while swimming with whales in Hawaii.

Absolutely! Did they have anything to protect themselves? Of course not! That is very, very typical. Sylvia has more guts than almost anybody you can name."

Sylvia's whale adventure was one of many she shared with her children. The family had moved to Oakland, California, where Sylvia conducted research through the California Academy of Sciences. Her second marriage had ended, and Sylvia felt sad about getting divorced again. Her own parents were still devoted to each other, and she admired their strong marriage. But it was as if Sylvia were wed to the sea, and her devotion and commitment lay there.

A humpback whale calf makes its way through the water.

Alice and Lewis often came to California to care for the children when Sylvia was on her expeditions. But sometimes Sylvia let the children stay out of school and go with her. Elizabeth, Richie, and Gale all learned how to scuba dive at a young age. When they were old enough, they helped the crew.

The whale project was one of these times. One day Elizabeth, who was 17, was given a big responsibility. She had to ride in the black rubber boat and take care of the expensive underwater cameras. When the crew needed a piece of equipment, she carefully handed it over the side. All of a sudden, the boat tipped up on one end. A whale was lifting the boat out of the water!

Elizabeth was shocked. "All around the boat was nothing but whales. It was like the whale was playing with the boat. I was so nervous—what would I do if the boat got tipped over?

I wasn't worried for me—the whales were so gentle—but I was supposed to be keeping the equipment dry!" Luckily the whale soon tired of this game and left her alone.

Sometimes the whales would sing their strange melodies, full of deep bass moans and high squeals. During the filming, Al Giddings was the first person ever to take a picture of humpbacks singing. As the whales sang, Sylvia and the children got into the water. The music was so loud and strong that it made their bodies tremble and vibrate from the sound waves—as if they were tiny mice shaking beside the pipes of a giant organ.

Sylvia aboard the boat on the whale mission in Hawaii

In the film *Gentle Giants of the Pacific,* Sylvia swims gracefully around the whales, her light brown hair streaming around her snorkel mask. The whales are just as graceful. Their tons of blubber do not keep them from smoothly gliding and twisting through the water, their powerful flukes churning clouds of foam.

Sylvia put the film to good use, showing it in 20 nations. Her audiences shared with her the thrill of seeing whales

Sylvia recording whale sounds

singing, romping, and caring for their young. Humpback whales, she said, swam in her dreams forever and brought a grin to her face when her mind wandered during a boring meeting. Getting to swim with such wonderful animals inspired her to speak out more strongly than ever on behalf of the critters who dwell in the seas.

When *Al Giddings* suggested to *Sylvia* that she take advantage of the opportunity to walk on the ocean floor, the plan at first seemed too dangerous to attempt.

EIGHT

A WILD AND CRAZY IDEA

In 1979, Al Giddings came to Sylvia with an idea for a new adventure. How would she like to take a walk in an aquasuit along the deep ocean floor while Al filmed her? Sylvia was skeptical. She had seen pictures of the suit Al had in mind. It was called a Jim suit, after Jim Jarrett, the diver who wore an earlier version of the suit in 1920. Divers wore the cumbersome Jim suit while they repaired oil rigs and performed other underwater chores.

Sylvia liked the freedom of moving through the water—almost like a bird flying through the air. She enjoyed gently touching the plants or sometimes even a fish. Wearing Jim underwater would be like dancing ballet in a suit of armor. Jim's pincerlike hands would probably crush a delicate piece of coral.

But Al was convinced that if people could see Sylvia walking on the ocean floor they would better understand the difficulties—and the promise—of deep-sea exploration. The footage from filming her walk could be used in the book *Exploring the Deep Frontier* and the television special on ocean exploration that he and Sylvia were working on for the National Geographic Society.

If she were willing, Sylvia would be the first scientist to use Jim. She began to like the idea. "The more I thought about it, the more intriguing the concept seemed. I could envision enormous advantages to being able to drop in on the ocean of my choice for a few minutes or hours, just as scientists go into a forest or desert—or into a laboratory—with Jim as an exotic but necessary lab coat," Sylvia wrote.

Al was not surprised that Sylvia was unable to resist the challenge. When had she ever said no to a deep-sea adventure? But for the plan to succeed, others had to be enlisted.

The first was Phil Nuytten of Oceaneering International, Inc., owner of all 15 Jim suits. He appreciated the idea that Jim might be useful to scientists. What Phil found especially exciting was that Sylvia would be using Jim in a new way. All previous Jim divers had been attached securely by a heavy cable to a platform on the surface of the water. Sylvia would be linked only by a slender 18-foot communications cord—not to the surface—but to a small underwater vehicle called a submersible, which would follow her as she walked. The submersible would allow her to go deeper in the ocean, perhaps to 1,500 feet, and she would be freer to explore. "Some might regard [this] as dancing too close to the edge of safe and sane diving," Sylvia wrote. "Phil and Al seemed uncommonly attracted to wild and crazy ideas."

Others were not so delighted. Graham Hawkes, a British marine engineer, was asked to judge the project's risks. Hawkes was concerned about the potential dangers. Still, after careful study, he determined that the expedition probably could be safely done.

The biggest hurdle was Dr. John Craven, director of the University of Hawaii's Marine Science Institute, who was responsible for *Star II,* the submersible that could transport

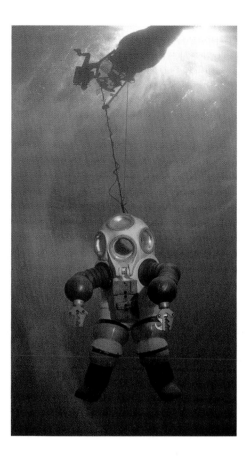

Jim hangs from the Star II *during a practice run.*

Sylvia to the bottom of the sea. Craven didn't hesitate. "No. Impossible. The risks are too great," he declared. But Hawkes managed to convince him otherwise.

The final task was raising money for the operation. Al and Sylvia patched together funds from National Geographic and other sources. When all was in place, preparations got under way for both Jim and Sylvia. Jim was taken apart and put back together again in an attempt to make it fit Sylvia's small frame. Hawkes worked to make Jim's joints more flexible in the deep ocean. Unlike a spacesuit, which Jim resembled, an aquasuit

Sylvia smiles through the head of the Jim suit.

must be made of tough material, such as ceramic or metal, or else the diver would be crushed under the pressure of the ocean. Jim was made of magnesium, a light, malleable metal. Its head and body were joined without a neck or waist, a design that made it look like an overweight white caterpillar. The suit's thick green arms had big round elbow and wrist joints and ended in wicked-looking steel pincers. The tree-trunk legs had round knee and hip joints and big black boots.

To put on the suit, Sylvia tilted the headpiece forward and climbed in from the top. Four round plastic portholes allowed her to look all around. Gauges inside the suit showed her the water's depth and the oxygen level. The suit's atmospheric pressure was the same as on land, so Sylvia did not have to go through a period of decompression.

For one week, Sylvia trained intensively, first in a big tank and then in shallow water near shore. Despite the weights being added to Jim's feet, she had to stand on her toes to walk. The suit was so big, she could easily move her arms to take notes. Lurching around the training tank, she said she felt like a drunken crab or a walking refrigerator.

At last all was ready. But as the time drew near, Al, perhaps feeling the burden of hatching this wild scheme, became increasingly nervous. One morning he fired questions at Sylvia: What if the suit leaks? What if the cord breaks and I can't pull you up? What if you get hung up on something and I can't get you free?

Sylvia simply got up and left the table. It was too late for second thoughts. Al would have to worry by himself about the dangers. Sylvia was ready to go.

Sylvia tries out the Jim suit.

NINE

THE JIM DIVE

As the tiny yellow submersible *Star II* descended into the Pacific Ocean on October 19, 1979, it carried a strange cargo. Strapped awkwardly around the waist and perched on a platform at the front of the sub was Sylvia, encased in the cumbersome Jim suit.

As the sub sank deeper, she focused intently on the constantly changing blue surrounding her. She wanted to remember every moment of this journey, the most dangerous and exciting of her life. For two-and-a-half hours she would walk across the deep ocean floor, where no human had ever stepped before.

Al Giddings and Bohdan (Bo) Bartko, one of the most experienced submersible pilots in the business, watched Sylvia from inside the sub. This was the third time Sylvia had packed her gear and tried the descent. Twice in the past week they had been forced to abandon the dive midway when a tiny copper wire snapped, and Sylvia and Al lost voice contact. This time, as Sylvia heard Al's voice saying they had reached one thousand feet, her hopes grew. Perhaps this would be the day.

The azure water turned to gray and then to midnight blue. Tiny glimmers of light sped by her helmet, like moths on a summer night. Her pulse quickened with excitement. At 1,150 feet under, Bo brought *Star II* down with a gentle bump on the sandy sea floor. In the glow of the headlights, Sylvia saw a white sponge, some slender branches of coral, and the glassy shells of red shrimp scurrying across the bottom. So eager was she to begin that she tried to take a step, forgetting she was still attached at the waist.

"How are Jim's joints?" Al asked. "Are you okay?"

Like the rusted Tin Man in *The Wizard of Oz,* Sylvia slowly tried to move Jim's limbs. The immense pressure of the sea made the suit's arms and legs stiff. She stomped the feet and flexed the elbows.

Though anxious to begin her explorations, she asked Bo to go deeper. She wanted to find a spot with more coral or rocks that would attract more fish. For another half hour, Bo guided the submersible. At last, at 1,250 feet, he said the time for searching was up. The sub's power supply was dwindling. Peering out at a marvelous seascape, Sylvia realized that they had found an ideal spot.

It was up to Al Giddings to turn the lever and release Sylvia—the most difficult thing he had done in all his 10 thousand dives. Every precaution had been taken, but the hazards were many. If Sylvia got into trouble at this depth, Al would be unable to safely leave the sub to help her.

He kept his voice calm as he asked Sylvia if she was ready to go. And Sylvia replied just as calmly, "Any time."

Al turned the handle, and a problem arose immediately. To Sylvia's dismay, Jim's toe was stuck on the platform of *Star II.* Could she be this close to her historic walk and have to scrap the mission?

The Jim suit

The mission was almost over before it began when the Jim suit became caught on the launcher.

Bo thought he could jar Sylvia loose by accelerating rapidly backward and forward. He shot the sub in reverse. After one try, the boot dislodged. At last Sylvia was free to roam—or as free as someone in a thousand-pound metal suit can be.

When Sylvia lumbered forward, she felt like Neil Armstrong taking the first dramatic step on the Moon. But unlike the barren moonscape, Sylvia discovered a world bustling with life, even at this crushing, sunless depth.

A dozen long-legged scarlet crabs—looking like colorful shirts hanging on a line to dry—clung to the branches of a delicate pink sea fan, a type of coral. Gleaming jellyfish drifted by like bubbles from a wand. Flat, diamond-shaped fish called rays—giant seven-foot specimens, larger than any she had ever seen—hovered off the ocean floor, rippling their rubbery wings.

Sylvia walks on the ocean floor.

As Sylvia walked, she jotted down her observations. A small cat shark (just 18 inches long) with emerald eyes glanced in her direction. The shark collided in seeming confusion with a stalk of coral, then glided away. Sylvia realized that *Star II's* lamps, dim to those who walk on land, must have seemed as bright as floodlights on a baseball field to creatures whose eyes had never gazed at the sun.

She asked Al to turn off the lights so she could better observe the bioluminescent creatures around her. Usually Al would have argued with her because without the lights he could not take pictures. But this time he obliged without protest.

Plunged suddenly into darkness, Sylvia's eyes took a few minutes to adjust. She thought of her family, who surely could not imagine her whereabouts at this moment. She had spared them the details of this dangerous dive.

Looking up through the top porthole of her suit, she was surprised to see an overarching blueness, like the dome of a heavenly cathedral. Even at this great depth, traveling through layer upon layer of water, the sun's powerful rays could be faintly seen, as at early dawn.

Accustomed now to the faint light, she focused on the bizarre and wonderful creatures around her. A lantern fish swam by, its even band of tiny yellow globes glowing warmly, like the windows of a passing train in the night. She stopped to watch a silvery hatchetfish, an extraordinary creature whose eyes perched on stalks, glaring upward, while its "headlights" beamed downward. She had seen this peculiar fish before, but only snagged in a net. Seeing it swim,

Sylvia came into contact with a lantern fish while exploring the ocean floor in the Jim suit.

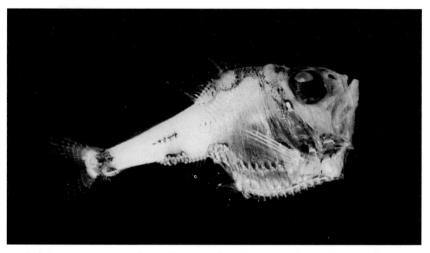

Sylvia was curious about the peculiar body design of the hatchetfish.

she wondered about its unusual design. Why had it evolved this way?

Suddenly a light show of blue burst out beside her. She was standing among hundreds of slender, coil-like colonies of bamboo coral. "The most gentle nudge of my claw provoked ring after ring of blue light to pulse . . . down the full length of the coral," she later wrote. When she touched the bottom stalk, the same light show occurred, with fiery blue dough-nut rings passing upward and through those rippling down.

Sylvia wrote furiously in her notebook. Her mind raced with questions. What purpose did the gleaming rings of blue serve? Were they a signal warning off other animals or a bea-con to attract prey? Her thoughts were interrupted by Al's voice telling her the time was up.

"You're kidding!" Sylvia cried. "It seems like 20 minutes." She slowly shuffled back to the sub and, using the Jim suit's pincers, took hold of two small flags, one U.S. and one

Sylvia emerges from the Jim suit after her historic walk.

representing National Geographic, that were attached to *Star II*. She planted the flags in the seabed, not to claim the area for the United States, but as a historic landmark of ocean exploration.

Reluctantly she told Al and Bo to begin the ascent. The sub rose slowly back through the changing shades of blue with Sylvia dangling from the cord. When she emerged, she took her place in the record books. The Jim suit would soon be replaced by advances in small submersibles. No one would again walk as deeply on the ocean floor as Sylvia had done.

Newspapers from around the world reported on the dive, and Al's pictures were printed in many books. Together Sylvia and Al produced a television special.

Sylvia remains a legend to many divers. Several years later, while she was investigating the effects of the *Exxon Valdez* oil spill in Alaska, a volunteer scuba diver emerged from the water. When he was introduced to Sylvia, he simply shouted, "Jim suit!"

Sylvia was happy that people thought the dive was significant, but what about all the incredible creatures she had seen? Weren't they even more extraordinary than her walk on the seafloor? When would the world share her thirst to discover not only life on other planets but the life right here on Earth?

The Deep Rover allowed Sylvia to go to depths of the ocean that had never been explored.

TEN

OCEAN EVEREST

Over the years, Sylvia had spent thousands of hours underwater, always learning something new. Her adventures continued to attract wide attention, but she was still not satisfied. Only once, in 1960, had two explorers gone to the deepest part of the ocean—seven miles down to the bottom of the Mariana Trench, east of the Philippine Islands. They used a submarinelike vessel, a bathyscaph, called *Trieste*. Yet as time went on, the government and universities spent less, not more, on underwater research. "To know that technologically we used to be able to travel to the ocean's greatest depths, but that presently we cannot, is a source of great frustration to me," Sylvia said.

More than 70 percent of Earth is covered with water—most of it in the oceans—yet less than one percent of the deep sea has been explored. New marine species are constantly being discovered. With more knowledge, Sylvia was convinced, people would better understand how all life depends on the sea.

Finally Sylvia decided she could wait no longer. She would find a way to advance ocean exploration herself. In 1981, she and engineer Graham Hawkes decided to become business partners. Their goal was to build one-person submersibles, small vehicles that could move through the ocean. They named their company Deep Ocean Technology (later called Deep Ocean Engineering).

Sylvia threw herself into the business with her usual enthusiasm. Graham Hawkes was president and chief engineer; Sylvia was vice president, secretary, treasurer, broom pusher, and whatever else needed doing.

With little money to start up the company, they ran the business out of Sylvia's home in Oakland, California. This was an even livelier time than usual in the household. The children were surrounded by discussions about the new enterprise. What should the submersibles be made of? Who would buy them? How could they raise money to purchase supplies and pay employees? Every table was covered with business plans and drawings of subs—which was the inspiration for the name "Blue Prints" for their black Labrador retriever puppy.

Blue Prints was not the only pet adding to the hubbub. Sylvia's house and yard were always filled with animals, just as her parents' home had been. There were cats, dogs, and at various times, geese, lizards, parrots, horses, guinea hens—even an orphan alligator found a foster home in the backyard pool.

Sylvia's father, Lewis, died in 1981 after an illness, but Alice often came for long visits. She brightened the serious discussions with her good humor and fresh baked cookies. At age 81, she even tried snorkeling for the first time.

Sylvia and Graham Hawkes found little interest in their idea for a crewed submersible. Until they could drum up more support, Hawkes came up with another plan. He de-

Sylvia's mother always supported her daughter's career. Sylvia and her mother are pictured here in 1987.

signed a large, remotely operated vehicle (ROV) that could be used to inspect undersea equipment. Finding the first customer was difficult, however. Underwater technology is expensive, and no one wanted to buy a new vehicle from an upstart company with no track record.

To Sylvia, the world of business seemed even less welcoming to women than the world of science had been. When she met with businessmen to try to convince them to invest in the new company or purchase the ROVs, she felt they looked down on her. "In business, men generally tend not to take women very seriously. They think we don't have a brain in our heads. Some are so arrogant you want to slug them!" she said.

Sylvia posed for a photograph with Deep Rover *while it was under construction.*

As the months went by, Sylvia and Graham worried that their company would fail. They finally sold one of their ROVs, named *Bandit,* to Shell Oil Company. Nine more orders followed.

In 1984, the company achieved its goal of producing a submersible that would hold people. *Deep Rover* was a small, round vehicle with mechanical arms. Made of clear acrylic, *Deep Rover* was like a sturdy bubble driven through the ocean.

This was a dream come true for Sylvia. Phil Nuytten, owner of the Jim suit, bought the first one. He, Sylvia, and

Sylvia tests Deep Rover.

Graham took turns taking *Deep Rover* to its greatest depth—three thousand feet—and they each set a new record for solo diving.

Sylvia took her turn at night. At one thousand feet, she suddenly heard whistles and clicks. Hundreds of dolphins were swimming above her. When she reached three thousand feet, the scene turned magical: "It was like falling into a fireworks display. Luminescent creatures sparkled and flashed with blue light."

Business improved the next year when Hawkes created a smaller, lightweight, easy to operate ROV called *Phantom.*

Graham Hawkes at the drawing board

Phantom was a big hit. One of the first customers was Disneyworld, which used *Phantom* to show visitors a fish-eye view of life inside a giant aquarium at Epcot's Living Seas Pavilion in Orlando, Florida.

Customers in more than 30 countries bought ROVs like *Phantom* to do all sorts of jobs, such as finding shipwrecks, checking for leaks in pipes, and diving under ice in the Antarctic. A few police departments even used *Phantom* as a detective to search for evidence (including dead bodies) dumped in the ocean.

After a few years, Sylvia and Graham's partnership turned romantic, and they were married in 1986. They decided to move the business out of their home and into a warehouse in nearby San Leandro. There they set up a small machine shop and testing tank.

Sylvia's life was still a whirlwind. The company's engineer, John Edwards, once said, "For years I thought she was a person who didn't need sleep. When she travels, her body doesn't recognize time zones. Now I know—she does sleep. Two hours a night!"

Sylvia's ultimate dream was what she and Graham called Ocean Everest. Just as climbing Mount Everest, the tallest

Sylvia and Graham edit underwater footage that was taken with one of their submersibles.

Sylvia has run across many interesting things in her diving career.

peak on land, was the dream of mountain climbers, Ocean Everest meant finding a new way to explore the deepest parts of the sea—much deeper than *Deep Rover* could go. "Ocean Everest is the code name for gaining access to our planet, from the inside out, from the ocean's greatest depths all the way back to the surface, and to do it with our own eyes, for long periods of time, so we can understand what's happening in the deep sea," she said.

Then in 1990, another unexpected opportunity came her way—one she hoped would lead to a new commitment to explore and protect the oceans.

Sylvia becomes a part of the sea when she dives.

ELEVEN

GUARDIAN OF THE SEA

Ever since Tektite, Sylvia had been frustrated with the government's lack of interest in sea exploration. In 1990 she had a chance to change that. President George H. W. Bush appointed Sylvia to be chief scientist at the National Oceanic and Atmospheric Administration (NOAA).

Sylvia felt honored to be asked. She would be the first woman ever to hold the position, but she wasn't sure she wanted to accept the job. As a high-level representative of the government, she would not be able to voice her own opinions to the media and the public. At last, however, she decided to give the job a try.

By this time, Sylvia's reputation had grown immensely. She had spent more than six thousand hours underwater, and she held many records for her dives. Other biologists had honored her by naming species after her—such as *Diadema sylvie,* a sea urchin, and *Pilina earli,* a red alga. The World Wildlife Fund, an important conservation organization, asked her to serve on its board of directors.

Sylvia was different from most scientists, who usually become an expert in only one area. Her interests extended beyond her specialty of algae to include the whole ecosystem of the ocean and its relationship to other life on Earth. "She's greatly respected for her very broad knowledge and her ability to put it all together into one big picture—the whole marine world," said shark expert Eugenie Clark. "She's constantly thinking, 'how does it all fit together,' and that's a wonderful way to look at it."

Many people who worked at NOAA were excited about Sylvia's appointment. "Somebody of her caliber gave a boost to the whole agency," recalled Joe Bishop, a senior scientist. "She was one of the most famous people to ever work for NOAA."

Her new job meant she had to move to Washington, D.C. It was a good time for her to leave California. Her children were grown. Once again, her marriage had ended in divorce, although she and Graham Hawkes continued to be business partners for a few more years before they both left the company. (She and her daughter Elizabeth later started a new company called Deep Ocean Exploration and Research.)

As NOAA's chief scientist, she went to many meetings and testified before Congress, but she also made time for expeditions. The most exciting one came in 1991, when the Japanese government invited her to go on a research dive in the three-person submersible called *Shinkai 6500*. Sylvia went far deeper than she had ever gone before—more than 13 thousand feet, or two and a half miles under—as deep as where the *Titanic* lay.

When she returned to Washington from Japan, Sylvia was more determined than ever to persuade the U.S. government to invest money in underwater research. She knew the gov-

Shinkai 6500 *allowed Sylvia to descend more than 13 thousand feet into the ocean—deeper than she had ever been before.*

ernment spent billions of dollars on satellites that looked down on the ocean and on a modern fleet of ships that sat on the surface of the sea, but only a small amount of money was spent on the study of underwater life. In fact, she often pointed out that the government spent more on the toilet for the space shuttle than on underwater research.

Yet as hard as she tried to make her case, she could not get government officials to agree that sea exploration was important. Getting them to increase funding was like trying to shove a whale. In February 1992, Sylvia resigned from NOAA, but before leaving, she carried out one last important mission.

In 1991 the United States and its allies had fought against Saddam Hussein, the leader of Iraq, during the Persian Gulf War. Iraq had set fire to hundreds of oil wells in the neighboring country of Kuwait, leaving a terrible environmental legacy. When millions of barrels of oil flowed into the Persian Gulf, scientists came from all over the world to study the damage and see what could be done. Sylvia was chief scientist of the underwater team of researchers.

When she arrived at the Persian Gulf one year after the war, she found a depressing scene. The landscape was blackened for miles. Diving into slick, brown waters, she found

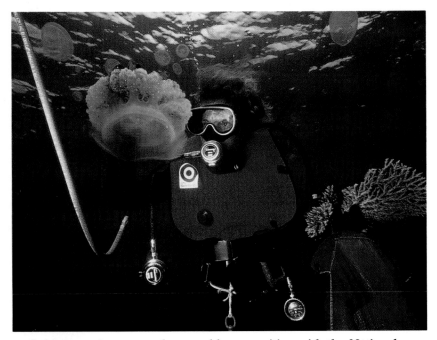

Sylvia's marine research earned her a position with the National Geographic Society.

crabs and birds smothered with black goo. Oil seeped deeply into the sand, forming an ugly pool. Even amid the terrible devastation, Sylvia saw reason to hope, however. Fresh young grass peeped through the tarry marshlands, tiny fish found shelter in sea shells, and burrowing crabs brought clean sand to the surface. Nature was struggling to heal itself.

Sylvia and the other scientists reported on what they'd found. Their research would be used to learn how long it would take life to recover in the Persian Gulf—if it ever does.

The more problems Sylvia witnessed in the oceans of the world, the more worried she became. Wherever she traveled, she found that life in the sea was in trouble. Trash and plastic bags from cruise ships smothered coral in once beautiful places like the Red Sea and the Indian Ocean. Huge fishing fleets dragged enormous nets and lines in the Atlantic and Pacific Oceans, taking so many fish that supplies are depleted before the fish can reproduce. Chemicals and sewage dumped into rivers eventually found their way to the sea, killing delicate plants and animals. The Gulf of Mexico that she had happily explored as a child was clouded with pollution, the sea grasses were gone—and with them many of the scallops, crabs, and sea horses.

"I didn't set out to be what is known as an environmentalist. But if you see things that you care about irreversibly destroyed, it's impossible not to do everything you can," she said. Sylvia would have liked nothing better than spending the rest of her life exploring the seas, swimming with whales, and identifying new critters, but she felt responsible for the world's oceans. To make others share her sense of urgency, she decided to spend more time on land, trying to reach people with her message.

She appeared on more than one hundred television

Sylvia at the Persian Gulf

programs, from *Mister Rogers' Neighborhood* to *Good Morning America.* (Mr. Rogers told his young viewers, "People like Sylvia Earle are my hero.") Many documentary films were made of her work. She lectured in 60 nations, and in 1996 she hosted *The Ocean Report,* a daily radio broadcast on the state of the seas. She wrote dozens of publications, including her 1995 book, *Sea Change: A Message of the Oceans,* that describes many of her adventures and the changes she has witnessed. Even after she became a grandmother, her hectic schedule never slowed.

The United Nations and President Bill Clinton designated 1998 as the Year of the Oceans. Sylvia was asked to spend the year as Explorer in Residence at the National Geographic Society. She planned to scuba dive at all of America's marine sanctuaries—national underwater parks where plants and animals are protected. She focused attention on the sanctuaries as one important tool for conserving life in the sea.

On one cold March morning in 1998, she stood in the auditorium of National Geographic headquarters in Washington, D.C. The room was filled with hundreds of school children who were part of the Jason Project, a high-tech experiment that linked students with biologists at work. Someone introduced Sylvia to the students as a record-breaking diver and scientist. At first the students were shy, but as Sylvia spoke, her enthusiasm seemed to spread. Soon dozens of hands wriggled in the air in hope of getting called on to ask a question.

"Is scuba diving similar to walking in space?" asked one girl.

"Have you ever been attacked by animals?"

"How big are giant squids?"

"Can hurricanes affect fish?"

"Have you ever seen a shark having a baby?"

"Actually, I have," Sylvia laughed, telling the students about her work in Eugenie Clark's lab. She urged the students to try exploring for themselves. "Anyone can put on that magic faceplate and go into the sea," she told them. "There is so much new to find. I hope you all can go there."

It is difficult for people to care about things that are unknown to them, Sylvia said. Only by exploring the sea will people understand why the marine world must be preserved.

Sometimes Sylvia grows discouraged about the future of the oceans, but she always finds some new reason to remain optimistic. Being with young people, seeing their curiosity and excitement, is to her one of the most hopeful signs of all.

Sources

8 Sylvia A. Earle, *Sea Change: A Message of the Oceans* (New York: G.P. Putnams Sons, 1995), 75.

13 Ibid., 40.

14 Alice Earle, interview with author, in Dunedin, Florida, January 1995.

14 Wallace White, "Her Deepness," *The New Yorker,* July 3, 1989, 50.

19 Sylvia Earle, interview with author, in Dunedin, Florida, January 1995.

19 Ibid.

19 Alice Earle interview, January 1995.

21 S. Earle interview, January 1995.

22 William Beebe, *Half-Mile Down,* (New York: Harcourt, Brace & Co., 1935), 10.

22 Sylvia Earle, phone interview with author, June 1995.

26 Beebe, *Half-Mile Down,* 72.

29 Earle, *Sea Change,* 45.

29 Ibid., 46.

30 Harold Humm, phone interview with author, March 1998.

30 S. Earle interview, January 1995.

30 Sylvia Earle, interview with author in Oakland, California, July 1995.

32 Ibid.

33 Ibid.

35 Ibid.

36 Earle, *Sea Change,* 56.

38 Ibid., 32.

38 Earle interview, July 1995.

Sylvia in her office in 1980

41 Eugenie Clark, phone interview with author, March 1998.

44 Earle, *Sea Change,* 68.

48 Sylvia A. Earle, "All-Girl Team Tests the Habitat," *National Geographic,* August 1971, 292.

49 Earle, *Sea Change,* 70.

51 Earle, *National Geographic,* August 1971, 291.

54 Earle, *Sea Change,* 69.

55 White, 56.

55 Sylvia Earle, interview with author in Washington, D.C., October 1993.

57 Sylvia A. Earle, "Humpbacks: The Gentle Whales," *National Geographic,* January 1979, 2.

58 Ibid., 2.

60 Roger Payne, phone interview with author, February 1998.

62 Elizabeth R. Taylor, phone interview with author, March 1998.

68 Earle, *Sea Change,* 103.

68 Ibid., 104.

69 Ibid., 105.

71 White, 60.

74 Earle, *Sea Change,* 107.

74 Sylvia A. Earle and Al Giddings, *Exploring the Deep Frontier: The Adventure of Man in the Sea* (Washington, DC: National Geographic Society, 1980), 231.

74 Sylvia A. Earle, "A Walk in the Deep," *National Geographic,* May 1980, 629.

79 Earle, *Sea Change,* 120.

79 Earle, *National Geographic,* May 1980, 631.

81 White, 46.

83 Earle interview, October 1993.

85 Earle interview, June 1995.

87 Ibid.

89 John Edwards interview with author in San Leandro, California, July 1995.

90 Earle interview, October 1993.

94 Clark interview.

94 Joe Bishop, phone interview with author, March 1998.

97 Earle interview, July 1995.

98 *Mr. Rogers' Neighborhood,* episode 1619, 1989.

99 Observed by author, March 1998.

Glossary

algae: plant or plantlike organisms usually found in water and commonly distinguished by color: green, red, yellow-green, brown, and blue-green

aquanaut: a scuba diver who lives and operates both inside and outside an underwater shelter for an extended period

bathysphere: a round steel diving device

bends: a sometimes fatal condition marked by pain, paralysis, and breathing distress due to the release of nitrogen bubbles in the bloodstream caused by too sudden a change in pressure, as when a diver ascends rapidly from the compressed atmosphere of the deep sea

bioluminescence: the emission of light from living organisms

blubber: the fat of whales and other large marine mammals

mouthpiece: the part of scuba gear that is inserted into the mouth to supply air to a diver underwater

rebreather: a device that recycles air for aquanauts by removing carbon dioxide chemically and adding oxygen from a tank as needed

scuba: (self-contained underwater breathing apparatus) gear that draws on a portable compressed-air supply at a regulated pressure to allow a diver to breathe while underwater

snorkel: a tube that extends above water and makes it possible for a person to breathe while swimming facedown in the water

submersible: a small underwater craft used especially for deep-sea research

Selected Bibliography

Selected Publications by Sylvia A. Earle

"Humpbacks: The Gentle Whales." *National Geographic,* January 1979.

"Life Springs from Death in Truk Lagoon." *National Geographic,* May 1976.

"Persian Gulf Pollution—Assessing the Damage One Year Later." *National Geographic,* February 1992.

"Science's Window on the Sea (part two): All-Girl Team Tests the Habitat." *National Geographic,* August 1971.

Sea Change: A Message of the Oceans. New York: G.P. Putnams Sons, 1995.

"Undersea World of a Kelp Forest." *National Geographic,* September 1980.

"A Walk in the Deep." *National Geographic,* May 1980.

With Al Giddings. *Exploring the Deep Frontier: The Adventure of Man in the Sea.* Washington, D.C.: National Geographic Society, 1980.

Books about Marine Life and Ocean Exploration

Beebe, William. *Half-Mile Down.* New York: Harcourt, Brace and Co., 1935.

Carson, Rachel. *The Sea Around Us.* New York: Oxford University Press, special edition, 1989.

Clark, Eugenie. *Lady with a Spear.* New York: Harper & Brothers, 1953.

Cousteau, Jacques-Yves, with Frederic Dumas. *The Silent World.* New York: Harper and Row Publishers, 1953.

Dover, Van, and Cindy Lee. *The Octopus's Garden: Hydrothermal Vents and Other Mysteries of the Deep Sea.* Reading, Mass.: Addison-Wesley Publishing Co., 1996.

Payne, Roger. *Among Whales.* New York: Charles Scribners Sons, 1995.

Piccard, Jacques, and Robert S. Dietz. *Seven Miles Down: The Story of the Bathyscaph Trieste.* New York: G.P. Putnams Sons, 1961.

Resources

Center for Marine Conservation
1725 DeSales Street
Washington, DC 20036
http://www.cmc-ocean.org

The Explorers Club
46 East 70th Street
New York, NY 10021
http://www.explorers.org

Marine Technology Society
1828 L Street, NW
Washington, DC 20036
http://www.cms.udel.edu/mts/

National Geographic Society
c/o Sustainable Seas Expeditions
1145 17th Street, NW
Washington, DC 20036
http://www.nationalgeographic.com/seas

National Marine Sanctuary Program
NOAA
1305 East-West Highway
Silver Spring, MD 20910
http://www.sanctuaries.noaa.gov

National Undersea Research
Program
1315 East-West Highway
Silver Spring, MD 20910
http://www.noaa.gov
http://www.uncwil.edu/nurc/

Sea Web
1731 Connecticut Avenue, NW
Washington, DC 10009
http://www.seaweb.org

Sustainable Seas Expeditions
735 State Street
Suite 305
Santa Barbara, CA 93101
http://www.nationalgeographic.com/seas

Other Titles in the Lerner Biographies Series

Agatha Christie

Allan Pinkerton

Babe Didrikson Zaharias

Billie Jean King

Charles Darwin

Charlie Chaplin

Douglas MacArthur

Dwight D. Eisenhower

E. B. White

Emily Dickinson

Frances Hodgson Burnett

Frank Lloyd Wright

George Balanchine

Gloria Steinem

J. M. Barrie

J. R. R. Tolkien

John Muir

Julia Morgan

L. Frank Baum

Laura Ingalls Wilder

Margaret Bourke-White

Maria Montessori

Marie Curie and Her
    Daughter Irène

Martin Luther King, Jr.

Mother Jones

Nellie Bly

Nikola Tesla

Rachel Carson

Robert Louis Stevenson

Sir Edmund Hillary

Index

Sylvia enjoys exploring the Bahamas in 1981.

Sylvia tests Deep Rover *in 1984.*

Sylvia in 1966 diving from a small boat in Jamaica

Photo Acknowledgments

The photographs are reproduced with the permission of: © Al Giddings/ Al Giddings Images, Inc., pp. 2, 64, 66, 75, 76, 77, 90, 92, 98; private collection of Sylvia Earle, pp. 6, 8, 10, 13, 15, 16, 18, 24, 28, 29, 34, 37, 39, 40, 42, 47, 51, 53, 54, 59, 63, 72, 80, 85, 86, 87, 96, 100, 106, 107, 108; © Bob Cranston, p. 20; © CORBIS/Hulton-Deutsch Collection, p. 21; © Doug Perrine/Innerspace Visions, pp. 26, 32, 56, 62; © Hulton-Getty/Liaison Agency, p. 27; © Daniel W. Gotshall/Visuals Unlimited, p. 31 (top); MPLIC, p. 31 (bottom); © OAR/ National Undersea Research Program, pp. 45, 49, 50, 82, 95; © Hal Beral/ Visuals Unlimited, p. 52; © David B. Fleetham/Tom Stack and Associates, p. 61; © Charles Nicklin/Al Giddings Images, Inc., p. 69; © Walt Clayton/ Al Giddings Images, Inc., p. 70; © G. Musil/Visuals Unlimited, p. 78; © Carré/Jacana/Photo Researchers, Inc., p. 79; © Roger Ressmeyer/ CORBIS, pp. 88, 89; © Ross Wells, p. 112.

Cover: © Al Giddings/Al Giddings Images, Inc.

Sylvia at her home in Oakland, California, in 1995

Author acknowledgments:
I wish to thank the many people who supported my dream of writing this book. My deepest appreciation goes to Sylvia Earle, who gave me many hours of her time for interviews in California, Washington, D.C., and Florida. I also am indebted to her family for their warmth and hospitality, especially her late mother, Alice, who kindly allowed me to interview her in her home in Dunedin, Florida, and Sylvia's daughter, Elizabeth, for all her help.

Greatly contributing to the book were the insights shared with me by Sylvia's colleagues over the years, including Eugenie Clark, Roger Payne, Joe Bishop, and Sylvia's mentor, Harold Humm.

Many others gave me input on the manuscript. Particularly helpful were the comments of young readers: my son, Danny; my niece, Carrie Lynn Wells; Caitlin Beane, Lizzie Coston, Katie McLaughlin, and Will Snider. Others who gave me advice and encouragement were Betty Baker, Barbara Carney, Frank Gallant, Leah Glasheen, Diane Holzheimer, Tawana Purnell, Ruth Wells, my daughter Sarah, and most of all my husband Ross Wells. Takoma Park children's librarian Jillian Herschberger also cheered me on throughout the project.

Finally, I wish to thank the AARP Bulletin for assigning me to write a profile on Sylvia Earle, thus giving me my first opportunity to meet someone whom I had long admired.

About the Author

Beth Baker is a freelance magazine writer with many interests, including biology, history, and the environment. She is an amateur naturalist, and she and her family enjoy snorkeling in the Florida Keys. She and her husband, Ross Wells, live in Takoma Park, Maryland, and have two children, Sarah and Danny.